D0519634

THIS WALKER BOOK BELONGS TO:

For Micky, Fred,
Iona, Mandala and Jackie
T. B.

For Patrick, Joe, Alicia, Lewis
and, of course, Tiziana
J. B-B.

Consultant: Martin Jenkins

First published 1998 by Walker Books Ltd
87 Vauxhall Walk, London SE11 5HJ

This edition published 2002

2 4 6 8 10 9 7 5 3 1

This book has been typeset in Veronan and Soupbone

Printed in Hong Kong

British Library Cataloguing in Publication Data:
a catalogue record for this book is
available from the British Library

ISBN 0-7445-6280-5

My Goose Betsy

Trudi Braun

illustrated by John Bendall-Brunello

WALKER BOOKS
AND SUBSIDIARIES
LONDON • BOSTON • SYDNEY

My goose Betsy has
smooth soft feathers
to keep her warm and dry,

wide webby feet to swim with,

and a long strong beak for tearing
at grass or pecking up corn.

This is how she walks —
in a stately waddle,
her long neck stretched out
and her head held high,
staring sideways out of
beady blue eyes.

This is how she talks —
with a squawk, or a honk, or a hiss.
She likes making lots of noise.

My goose Betsy is building
a nest for her eggs.

Carefully, carefully,
she collects straw
with her beak

and makes a big heap
in the corner of the
goose house.

She sits on the heap
and shuffles her bottom
around to make
a snug hollow.

She lines it with fluffy down,
which she pecks from her breast.

When the nest is cosy and soft,
she lays her first egg.

Every two days
Betsy lays another egg,
until her nest is full.

Then she settles down on top
to keep the eggs warm until they hatch.

Day
after day
she sits very
still in the quiet
dark goose house.

Outside William the gander
is standing guard.
If anyone comes near
he hurries towards them,
his wings spread,
his neck outstretched...

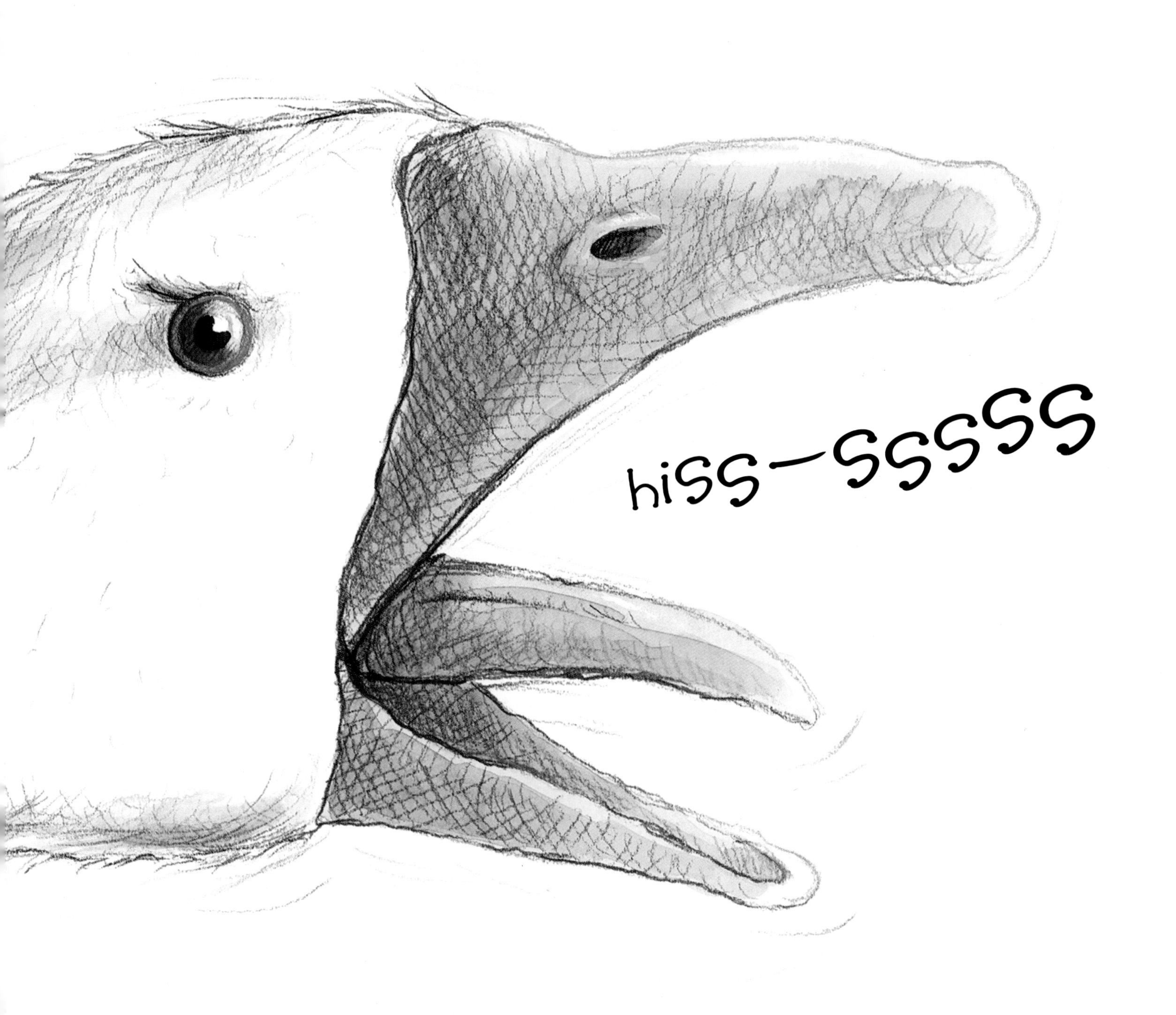

and his beak open wide
in a fierce hiss–sssss.

Once a day only,
Betsy gets off her nest.
Out she runs,
calling to the gander.

She stands on one leg,
stretching the other
out behind her
like a ballerina...

and spreads her wings
— a lovely slow stretch.

Then she pecks at some grass,
and has a quick splash
in the water tub.

But soon she hurries back to
her eggs before they get cold.

All the time Betsy is sitting
on her nest, her goslings
are growing inside
the eggs…

until one day,
the first gosling
is ready to hatch.

It begins to tap with its beak against
the hard eggshell,
and the shell
starts to
break.

The gosling taps some more.
The shell cracks open.

Now the gosling
starts to push
with its legs.

Tap, tap, tap.
Push, push, push.
What a struggle!

Suddenly it is free.
The eggshell falls away
and the gosling
tumbles
out into
the world,
out into the soft warm nest,
where Betsy is waiting
to gather it up under her wing.

One by one all the eggs break
open, until her nest is full
of fluffy yellow babies.

My goose Betsy is a mother goose.

A few more GOOSE facts

The farmyard geese in this story are Embdens. They're descended from a kind of wild goose called the Greylag.

Laying eggs

Geese lay their eggs in spring. They're white and about three times as big as hens' eggs.

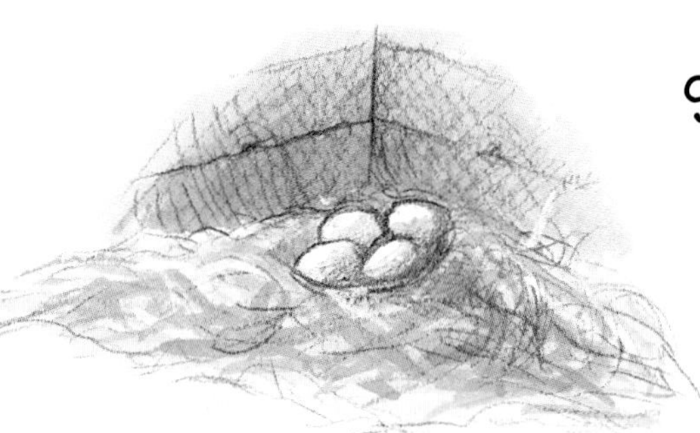

Sitting on the nest

A goose will usually start to sit on her nest when she's laid eight to twelve eggs. It takes thirty days for them to hatch.

Inside the eggs

A gosling starts off as a tiny dot inside an egg. It feeds on the yolk as it grows, and by hatching time its body almost fills the egg.

Newborn goslings

A newly hatched gosling doesn't need to eat or drink — it just stays in the nest and is kept warm by its mother. After a few days, she takes all her goslings outside to find grass and water.

Growing up

Goslings are covered in fluffy yellow down at first, and start to grow white feathers when they're about a month old. After one year, they're ready to lay eggs and have babies of their own. Geese live for as long as thirty years.

Index

Look up the pages to find out about all these geese things.

About the Author

Trudi Braun's own geese William and Dorothy came to live with her in Northumberland when they were one-week-old goslings. They are now twelve years old and great grandparents. She still feels especially close to her first pets, though today she has hens, cats, horses, sheep and three children as well. She has wanted to write a book ever since she was a little girl, but this is the first one ever to get finished.

About the Illustrator

John Bendall-Brunello says that illustrating this book gave him the chance to call upon childhood memories of visits to his great aunt, who kept a cow, a goat, four pigs, and a great gaggle of turkeys, ducks, chickens and geese. John's other picture books for Walker include *When I Grow Bigger* by Trish Cooke, *Easy Peasy!* by Sarah Hayes, and *The Big Bad Mole's Coming* and *Yum, Yum, Yummy* by Martin Waddell.

NOTES FOR TEACHERS

The READ AND WONDER series is an innovative and versatile resource for reading, thinking and discovery. Each book invites children to become excited about a topic, see how varied information books can be, and want to find out more.

READ AND WONDER

Reading aloud The story form makes these books ideal for reading aloud – in their own right or as part of a cross-curricular topic, to a child or to a whole class. After you've introduced children to the books in this way, they can revisit and enjoy them again and again.

Shared reading Big Book editions are available for several titles, so children can read along, discuss the topic, and comment on the different ways information is presented – to wonder together.

Group and guided reading Children need to experience a range of reading materials. Information books like these help develop the skills of reading to learn, as part of learning to read. With the support of a reading group, children can become confident, flexible readers.

Paired reading It's fun to take turns to read the information in the main text or captions. With a partner, children can explore the pages to satisfy their curiosity and build their understanding.

Individual reading These books can be read for interest and pleasure by children at home and in school.

Research Once children have been introduced to these books through reading aloud, they can use them for independent or group research, as part of a curricular topic.

Children's own writing You can offer these books as strong models for children's own information writing. They can record their observations and findings about a topic, make field notes and sketches, and add extra snippets of information for the reader.

Above all, Read and Wonders are to be enjoyed, and encourage children to develop a lasting curiosity about the world they live in.

Sue Ellis, Centre for Language in Primary Education